FAMOUS KEYBOARD INTROS

ISBN-13: 978-0-634-02656-0
ISBN-10: 0-634-02656-9

HAL•LEONARD®
CORPORATION
7777 W. BLUEMOUND RD. P.O. BOX 13819 MILWAUKEE, WI 53213

Visit Hal Leonard Online at
www.halleonard.com

CONTENTS

Against All Odds
(Take a Look at Me Now)

Words and Music by Phil Collins

Track 1

Artist: Phil Collins

Album: *Against All Odds* Motion Picture Soundtrack

Year: 1984

Keyboardist: Rob Mounsey

Trivia: This #1 hit, originally titled "How Can You Just Sit There?", was left over from the recording sessions for Collins's first solo album, *Face Value*. Collins won the GRAMMY® for Best Male Pop Vocal Performance in 1985, and was nominated for an Oscar for Best Song, but the Academy did not allow him to perform the song during the awards show (it was performed by actress Ann Reinking.)

Alone

Words and Music by Billy Steinberg and Tom Kelly

Track 2

Artist: Heart

Album: *Bad Animals*

Year: 1987

Keyboardist: Nancy Wilson

Trivia: This song was originally released on an album titled *Taking a Cold Look* from songwriters Billy Steinberg and Tom Kelly's i-Ten project in 1983. Steinberg was unhappy with the album and forgot about the songs until they heard Heart was looking to record a power ballad and Kelly suggested giving them "Alone." The song was a #1 hit.

Bennie and the Jets

Words and Music by Elton John and Bernie Taupin

Track 3

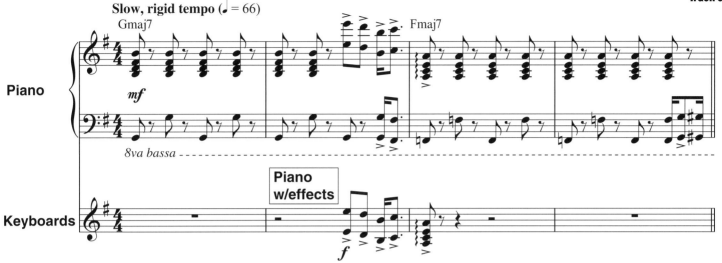

Artist: Elton John
Album: *Goodbye Yellow Brick Road*
Year: 1973
Keyboardist: Elton John

Trivia: This #1 hit, which Elton John did not want to release as a single, appeared on the list of songs deemed inappropriate by Clear Channel following the September 11, 2001 terrorist attacks (read: "bin Laden and the Jets.")

Bloody Well Right

Words and Music by Rick Davies and Roger Hodgson

Track 4

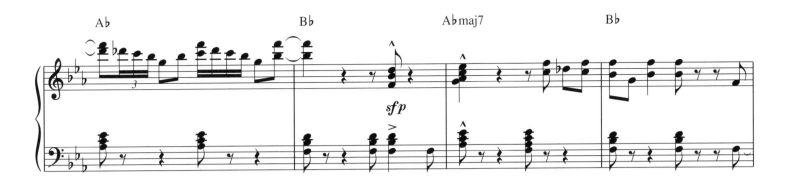

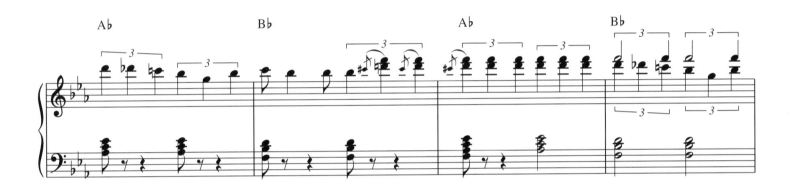

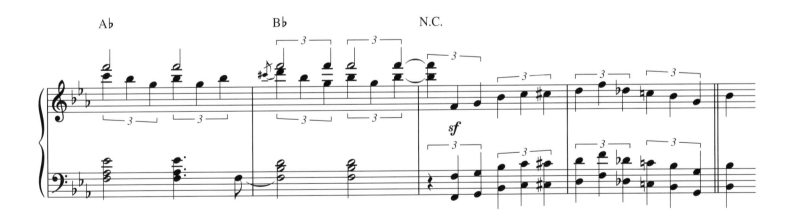

Artist: Supertramp	**Trivia:** Supertramp's 1980 hit "Dreamer," which peaked at #15, was the B-side of this single in 1975.
Album: *Crime of the Century*	
Year: 1974	
Keyboardist: Rick Davies	

Brick

Words and Music by Ben Folds and Darren Jessee

Artist: Ben Folds Five
Album: *Whatever and Ever Amen*
Year: 1997
Keyboardist: Ben Folds

Trivia: It is well-known that this #19 hit is the autobiographical story of Ben Folds's high school girlfriend getting an abortion, however, Ben originally was secretive about the meaning of this song. During a *Raleigh News & Observer* interview published in 1998 he loosely stated that the song's lyrics were based on a personal experience, and later was granted permission from his high school girlfriend to discuss the song's subject matter in more detail.

Clocks

Words and Music by Guy Berryman, Jon Buckland, Will Champion and Chris Martin

Track 6

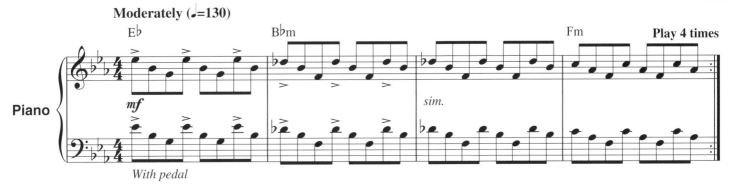

Artist: Coldplay **Album:** *A Rush of Blood to the Head* **Year:** 2002 **Keyboardist:** Chris Martin	**Trivia:** Though this song was added to the *A Rush of Blood to the Head* album at the last minute, the single won the GRAMMY for Record of the Year in 2004.

(They Long to Be) Close to You

Track 7

Lyric by Hal David
Music by Burt Bacharach

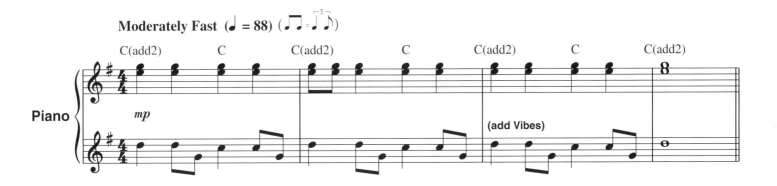

Artist: Carpenters **Album:** *Close to You* **Year:** 1970 **Keyboardist:** Richard Carpenter	**Trivia:** This song, which was #1 for four weeks in 1970, was ranked #193 in the Songs of the Century educational project conducted by the Recording Industry Association of America, the National Endowment for the Arts, and Scholastic Inc. in 2001.

Cold as Ice

Words and Music by Mick Jones and Lou Gramm

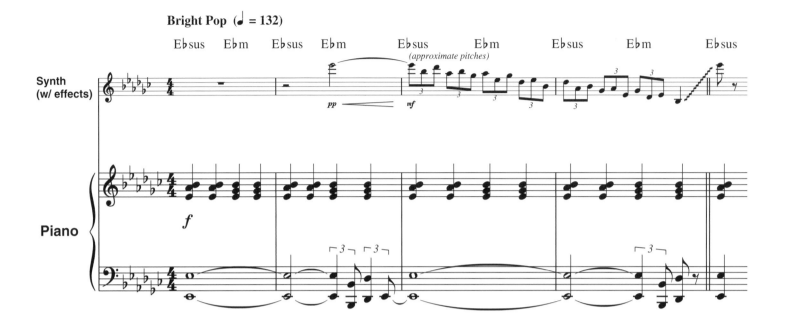

Artist: Foreigner **Album:** *Foreigner* **Year:** 1977 **Keyboardist:** Alan Greenwood	**Trivia:** This band's songs were the subject of a 2002 episode of *Aqua Teen Hunger Force* when the extraterrestrial Mooninite characters acquired the magical Foreigner Belt that gave the holder super-powers based on the lyrics to some of the band's hits. When "Cold as Ice" was activated the human character Carl was frozen solid.

Come Sail Away

Words and Music by Dennis DeYoung

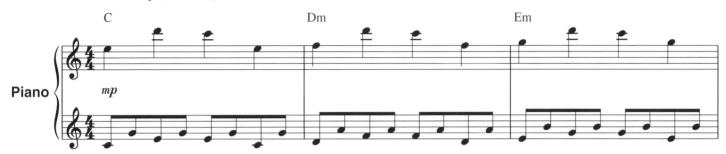

Artist: Styx
Album: *The Grand Illusion*
Year: 1977
Keyboardist: Dennis DeYoung

Trivia: This #8 hit has been featured in or referred to on television shows such as *South Park*, *Freaks and Geeks*, *ER*, *Ed*, and *Family Guy*.

Crazy

Words and Music by Willie Nelson

Track 10

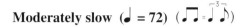

Piano, organ, guitar and bass arranged for piano

Artist: Patsy Cline
Album: *Showcase with the Jordanaires*
Year: 1961
Keyboardist: Floyd Cramer

Trivia: This song was originally to be recorded by Cline's friend, country singer Billy Walker, who turned it down to record another Willie Nelson song. Patsy didn't care for "Crazy," which would turn out to be her biggest hit, or her previous hits "Walkin' After Midnight" and "I Fall to Pieces."

Dream On

Words and Music by Steven Tyler

Track 11

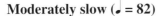

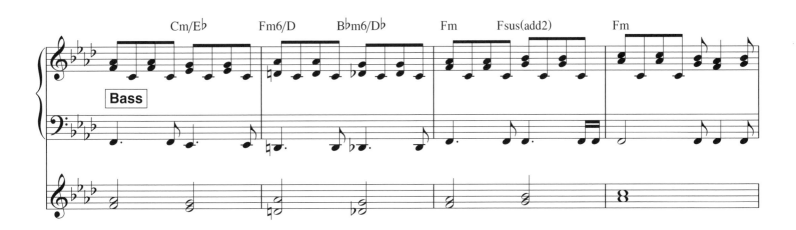

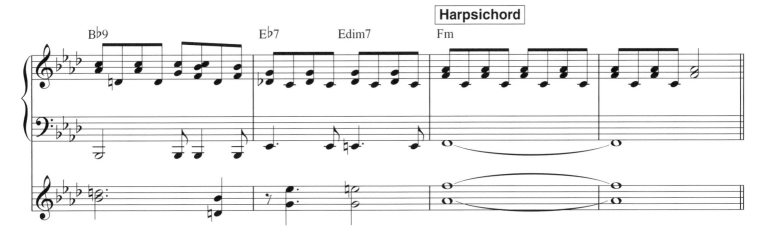

Artist: Aerosmith

Album: *Aerosmith*

Year: 1973

Keyboardist: Steven Tyler

Trivia: This song was sampled for Eminem's "Sing for the Moment," covered by Andru Donalds and Ronnie James Dio with Yngwie J. Malmsteen, and appears in the films *Miracle* (2004) and *Last Action Hero* (1993.)

Easy
Words and Music by Lionel Richie

Track 12

Artist: Commodores
Album: *Commodores*
Year: 1977
Keyboardist: Milan Williams

Trivia: This #4 hit has been covered by blind soul singer Clarence Carter, Irish boy band Westlife, Faith No More, and was sampled for "Six Feet Deep" by Geto Boys.

Hero
Words and Music by Mariah Carey and Walter Afanasieff

Track 14

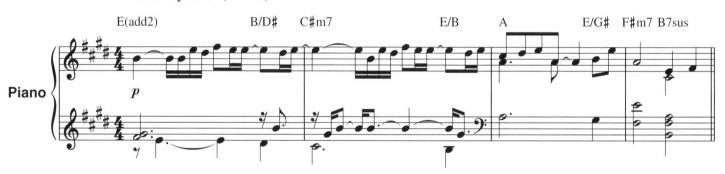

Artist: Mariah Carey
Album: *Music Box*
Year: 1993
Keyboardist: Walter Afanasieff

Trivia: The producers of the 1992 film *Hero* had asked Mariah and co-writer Walter Afanasieff to write a song for the movie's soundtrack that would be recorded by Gloria Estefan (the filmmakers later decided not to use it.) After hearing the song, Sony/Columbia Records executive Tommy Mottola (who would later become Carey's husband) encouraged her to keep it for herself. Carey was hesitant, as she felt the lyrics were intended for someone else to sing. The song was a #1 hit.

Hard to Say I'm Sorry

Words and Music by Peter Cetera and David Foster

Track 13

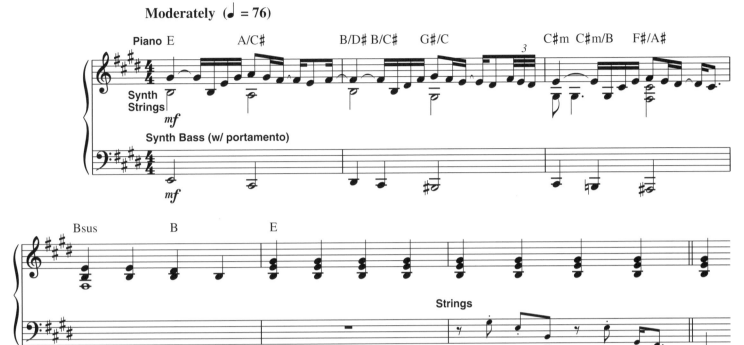

Artist: Chicago

Album: *Chicago 16*

Year: 1982

Keyboardist: Robert Lamm

Trivia: The album version of this #1 hit segued into a song called "Get Away," which was added in an effort to please longtime fans who preferred the band's previous uptempo material that featured the horn section. Most radio stations did not play the entire album track when the single was popular, but more recently the complete track has received airplay.

(Everything I Do) I Do It for You

from the Motion Picture ROBIN HOOD: PRINCE OF THIEVES

Words and Music by Bryan Adams, R.J. Lange and Michael Kamen

Track 15

Artist: Bryan Adams

Album: *Robin Hood: Prince of Thieves* soundtrack, *Waking Up the Neighbours*

Year: 1991

Keyboardist: Bill Payne

Trivia: This "royal" hit was supposed to be recorded by another artist for *Robin Hood: Prince of Thieves*, and the film company and score composer Michael Kamen didn't like what Adams and co-writer Robert "Mutt" Lange wrote. Adams refused to change it, so the song was stuck at the film's ending credits. After being released as a single, the song spent 7 weeks at the top of the U.S. chart, a lengthy 39 weeks at #1 in Adams's homeland of Canada, and topped many European charts as well.

I Write the Songs

Words and Music by Bruce Johnston

Artist: Barry Manilow
Album: *Tryin' to Get the Feeling*
Year: 1975
Keyboardists: Barry Manilow (piano), Alan Axelrod (keyboard)

Trivia: Barry Manilow was hesitant to record this song, which was written by Beach Boy Bruce Johnston, in fear that the listeners would think it was about his songs. The song is actually about music itself, and was a #1 hit.

Imagine

Words and Music by John Lennon

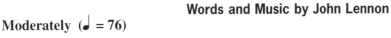

Artist: John Lennon and the Plastic Ono Band
Album: *Imagine*
Year: 1971
Keyboardist: John Lennon

Trivia: According to former President Jimmy Carter, this pro-peace song's status is almost equal to a national anthem in many countries. However, that didn't stop it from being included on the list of songs deemed inappropriate by Clear Channel following the September 11, 2001 terrorist attacks.

It's Too Late

Words and Music by Carole King and Toni Stern

Artist: Carole King

Album: *Tapestry*

Year: 1971

Keyboardist: Carole King

Trivia: This #1 hit was a double A-side single with King's song "I Feel the Earth Move" and won the GRAMMY for Record of the Year in 1972.

Just Once

Words by Cynthia Weil
Music by Barry Mann

Track 20

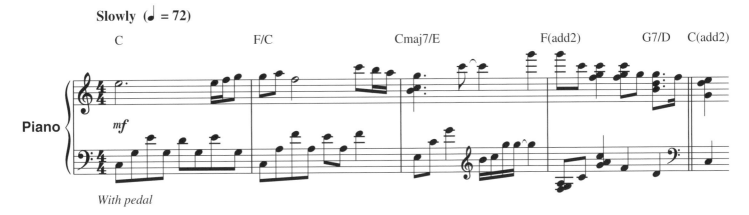

Artist: Quincy Jones featuring James Ingram **Album:** *The Dude* **Year:** 1981 **Keyboardist:** Robbie Buchanan	**Trivia:** Vocalist James Ingram won a GRAMMY in 1981 for Best Male R&B Vocal Performance for his work on the track "One Hundred Ways," also off Quincy Jones's album *The Dude*.

Let It Be

Words and Music by John Lennon and Paul McCartney

Track 21

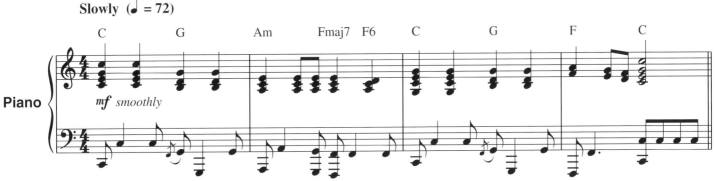

Artist: The Beatles **Album:** *Let It Be* **Year:** 1970 **Keyboardist:** Paul McCartney (organ played by Billy Preston)	**Trivia:** This #1 hit, which was ranked at #20 on *Rolling Stone's* list of the 500 Greatest Songs of All Time, was inspired by a dream Paul McCartney had about his mother who had died when he was 14. It is not about the Virgin Mary as some may interpret the song's lyrics.

Jump

Words and Music by David Lee Roth, Edward Van Halen, Alex Van Halen and Michael Anthony

Artist: Van Halen
Album: *1984*
Year: 1984
Keyboardist: Eddie Van Halen

Trivia: "Jump" was Van Halen's only #1 hit, and was the first song to be recorded in Eddie Van Halen's 5150 studio. Though it was rather low-budget, the video, directed by David Lee Roth, won the award for Best Stage Performance Video at the 1984 MTV Video Music Awards.

Louie, Louie

Words and Music by Richard Berry

Artist: Kingsmen

Album: *The Kingsmen in Person*

Year: 1963

Keyboardist: Don Gallucci

Trivia: The Kingsmen's version of this song sparked controversy in the 1960s, as parents across the country thought that the practically unintelligible lyrics must be profane. The FBI even conducted a 31-month investigation of the song, but concluded that they were "unable to interpret any of the wording in the record," so it was impossible to determine if the content was in violation of obscenity laws.

Takin' It to the Streets

Words and Music by Michael McDonald

Artist: The Doobie Brothers

Album: *Takin' It to the Streets*

Year: 1976

Keyboardist: Michael McDonald (organ played by Jesse Butler)

Trivia: This song was covered by American Idol Taylor Hicks as the B-side to his single "Do I Make You Proud." He also performed the song on the television show.

100 Years

Words and Music by John Ondrasik

Artist: Five for Fighting
Album: *The Battle for Everything*
Year: 2004
Keyboardist: John Ondrasik

Trivia: This #1 Adult Contemporary hit has been featured in the television shows *Smallville, Scrubs, Clubhouse, JAG,* and a commercial for financial services company JPMorgan Chase.

Piano Man

Words and Music by Billy Joel

Artist: Billy Joel
Album: *Piano Man*
Year: 1973
Keyboardist: Billy Joel

Trivia: Columbia Records executives felt that this song, clocking in at 5:38, was too long to be released as a single without being shortened. Joel retold this story in his song "The Entertainer."

Superstition

Words and Music by Stevie Wonder

Moderately (♩ = 100)

Multiple clavinet tracks arranged as one

Artist: Stevie Wonder
Album: *Talking Book*
Year: 1972
Keyboardist: Stevie Wonder

Trivia: This #1 hit was originally intended for Jeff Beck, but Wonder's manager insisted he record it instead. Beck, however, did play guitar on the *Talking Book* album and later released a version of "Superstition" on his studio album with Beck, Bogert & Appice.

Walking in Memphis

Words and Music by Marc Cohn

Artist: Marc Cohn
Album: *Marc Cohn*
Year: 1991
Keyboardist: Marc Cohn

Trivia: Thanks to this song, Marc Cohn, whose former band the Supreme Court was discovered by singer/songwriter Carly Simon, won the GRAMMY for Best New Artist in 1991.

Werewolves of London

Words and Music by Warren Zevon, Robert Wachtel and LeRoy Marinel

Artist: Warren Zevon
Album: *Excitable Boy*
Year: 1978
Keyboardist: Warren Zevon

Trivia: This song would have been appropriate for the soundtrack to the 1981 film *An American Werewolf in London*, but director John Landis was unable to license the song. Perhaps it wouldn't have made the cut because the songs that did appear in the movie all happen to have "moon" in the title.

A Whiter Shade of Pale

Words and Music by Keith Reid and Gary Brooker

Track 29

*Organ and bass arranged for organ

Artist: Procol Harum

Album: *Procol Harum*

Year: 1967

Keyboardist: Gary Brooker
(organ played by Matthew Fisher)

Trivia: This song, whose organ riff is loosely based on J.S. Bach's "Air on the G String" and "Sleepers, Awake," comes in at #57 on *Rolling Stone's* list of the 500 Greatest Songs of All Time.

You Are So Beautiful

Words and Music by Billy Preston and Bruce Fisher

Moderately slow (♩ = 60)

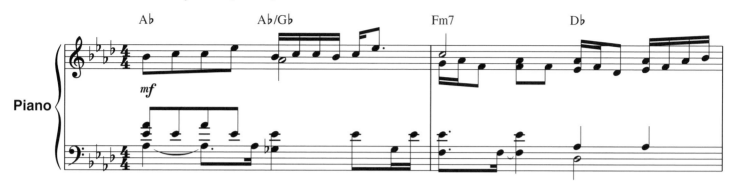

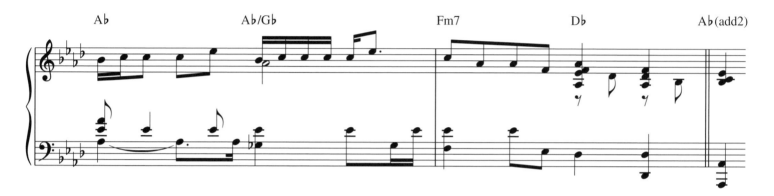

Artist: Joe Cocker
Album: *I Can Stand a Little Rain*
Year: 1974
Keyboardist: Nicky Hopkins

Trivia: It is said that Beach Boy Dennis Wilson helped this song's co-writer, Billy Preston, finish this song while the two were hanging out at a party. Wilson never sought any credit for his contribution, but he had performed it live between 1975-1983.

NOTE-FOR-NOTE KEYBOARD TRANSCRIPTIONS

These outstanding collections feature note-for-note transcriptions from the artists who made the songs famous.
No matter what style you play, these books are perfect for performers or students who want to play just like their keyboard idols.

ACOUSTIC PIANO BALLADS

16 acoustic piano favorites: Angel • Candle in the Wind • Don't Let the Sun Go Down on Me • Endless Love • Imagine • It's Too Late • Let It Be • Mandy • Ribbon in the Sky • Sailing • She's Got a Way • So Far Away • Tapestry • You Never Give Me Your Money • You've Got a Friend • Your Song.

00690351 / $19.95

ELTON JOHN

18 of Elton John's best songs: Bennie and the Jets • Candle in the Wind • Crocodile Rock • Daniel • Don't Let the Sun Go Down on Me • Goodbye Yellow Brick Road • I Guess That's Why They Call It the Blues • Little Jeannie • Rocket Man • Your Song • and more!

00694829 / $20.95

THE BEATLES KEYBOARD BOOK

23 Beatles favorites, including: All You Need Is Love • Back in the U.S.S.R. • Come Together • Get Back • Good Day Sunshine • Hey Jude • Lady Madonna • Let It Be • Lucy in the Sky with Diamonds • Ob-La-Di, Ob-La-Da • Oh! Darling • Penny Lane • Revolution • We Can Work It Out • With a Little Help from My Friends • and more.

00694827 / $20.95

THE CAROLE KING KEYBOARD BOOK

16 of King's greatest songs: Beautiful • Been to Canaan • Home Again • I Feel the Earth Move • It's Too Late • Jazzman • (You Make Me Feel) Like a Natural Woman • Nightingale • Smackwater Jack • So Far Away • Sweet Seasons • Tapestry • Way Over Yonder • Where You Lead • Will You Love Me Tomorrow • You've Got a Friend.

00690554 / $19.95

CLASSIC ROCK

35 all-time rock classics: Beth • Bloody Well Right • Changes • Cold as Ice • Come Sail Away • Don't Do Me like That • Hard to Handle • Heaven • Killer Queen • King of Pain • Layla • Light My Fire • Oye Como Va • Piano Man • Takin' Care of Business • Werewolves of London • and more.

00310940 / $24.95

POP/ROCK

35 songs, including: Africa • Against All Odds • Axel F • Centerfold • Chariots of Fire • Cherish • Don't Let the Sun Go Down on Me • Drops of Jupiter (Tell Me) • Faithfully • It's Too Late • Just the Way You Are • Let It Be • Mandy • Sailing • Sweet Dreams Are Made of This • Walking in Memphis • and more.

00310939 / $24.95

JAZZ

24 favorites from Bill Evans, Thelonious Monk, Oscar Peterson, Bud Powell, Art Tatum and more. Includes: Ain't Misbehavin' • April in Paris • Autumn in New York • Body and Soul • Freddie Freeloader • Giant Steps • My Funny Valentine • Satin Doll • Song for My Father • Stella by Starlight • and more.

00310941 / $22.95

R&B

35 R&B classics: Baby Love • Boogie on Reggae Woman • Easy • Endless Love • Fallin' • Green Onions • Higher Ground • I'll Be There • Just Once • Money (That's What I Want) • On the Wings of Love • Ribbon in the Sky • This Masquerade • Three Times a Lady • and more.

00310942 / $24.95

THE BILLY JOEL KEYBOARD BOOK

16 mega-hits from the Piano Man himself: Allentown • And So It Goes • Honesty • Just the Way You Are • Movin' Out • My Life • New York State of Mind • Piano Man • Pressure • She's Got a Way • Tell Her About It • and more.

00694828 / $22.95

STEVIE WONDER

14 of Stevie's most popular songs: Boogie on Reggae Woman • Hey Love • Higher Ground • I Wish • Isn't She Lovely • Lately • Living for the City • Overjoyed • Ribbon in the Sky • Send One Your Love • Superstition • That Girl • You Are the Sunshine of My Life • You Haven't Done Nothin'.

00306698 / $21.95

Prices, contents and availability subject to change without notice.

FOR MORE INFORMATION, SEE YOUR LOCAL MUSIC DEALER,
OR WRITE TO:

HAL•LEONARD® CORPORATION
7777 W. BLUEMOUND RD. P.O. BOX 13819 MILWAUKEE, WI 53213

Visit Hal Leonard online at www.halleonard.com

0107

KEYBOARD *signature licks*

These exceptional book/CD packs teach keyboardists the techniques and styles used by popular artists from yesterday and today. Each folio breaks down the trademark riffs and licks used by these great performers.

BEST OF BEBOP PIANO
by Gene Rizzo

16 bebop piano transcriptions: April in Paris • Between the Devil and the Deep Blue Sea • I Don't Stand a Ghost of a Chance • If I Were a Bell • Lullaby of Birdland • On a Clear Day (You Can See Forever) • Satin Doll • Thou Swell • and more.
00695734..$19.95

CONTEMPORARY CHRISTIAN
by Todd Lowry

Learn the trademark keyboard styles and techniques of today's top contemporary Christian artists. 12 songs, including: Fool for You (Nichole Nordeman) • The Great Divide (Point of Grace) • His Strength Is Perfect (Steven Curtis Chapman) • How Beautiful (Twila Paris) • If I Stand (Rich Mullins) • Know You in the Now (Michael Card) • and more.
00695753...............................$19.95

BILL EVANS
by Brent Edstrom

12 songs from pianist Bill Evans, including: Five • One for Helen • The Opener • Peace Piece • Peri's Scope • Quiet Now • Re: Person I Knew • Time Remembered • Turn Out the Stars • Very Early • Waltz for Debby • 34 Skidoo.
00695714...............................$22.95

BEN FOLDS FIVE
by Todd Lowry

16 songs from four Ben Folds Five albums: Alice Childress • Battle of Who Could Care Less • Boxing • Brick • Don't Change Your Plans • Evaporated • Kate • The Last Polka • Lullabye • Magic • Narcolepsy • Philosophy • Song for the Dumped • Underground.
00695578..$22.95

BILLY JOEL CLASSICS: 1974-1980
by Robbie Gennet

15 popular hits from the '70s by Billy Joel: Big Shot • Captain Jack • Don't Ask Me Why • The Entertainer • Honesty • Just the Way You Are • Movin' Out (Anthony's Song) • My Life • New York State of Mind • Piano Man • Root Beer Rag • Say Goodbye to Hollywood • Scenes from an Italian Restaurant • She's Always a Woman • The Stranger.
00695581..$22.95

BILLY JOEL HITS: 1981-1993
by Todd Lowry

15 more hits from Billy Joel in the '80s and '90s: All About Soul • Allentown • And So It Goes • Baby Grand • I Go to Extremes • Leningrad • Lullabye (Goodnight, My Angel) • Modern Woman • Pressure • The River of Dreams • She's Got a Way • Tell Her About It • This Is the Time • Uptown Girl • You're Only Human (Second Wind).
00695582..$22.95

ELTON JOHN CLASSIC HITS
by Todd Lowry

10 of Elton's best are presented in this book/CD pack: Blue Eyes • Chloe • Don't Go Breaking My Heart • Don't Let the Sun Go Down on Me • Ego • I Guess That's Why They Call It the Blues • Little Jeannie • Sad Songs (Say So Much) • Someone Saved My Life Tonight • Sorry Seems to Be the Hardest Word.
00695688..$22.95

LENNON & MCCARTNEY HITS
by Todd Lowry

Features 15 hits from A-L for keyboard by the legendary songwriting team of John Lennon and Paul McCartney. Songs include: All You Need Is Love • Back in the U.S.S.R. • The Ballad of John and Yoko • Because • Birthday • Come Together • A Day in the Life • Don't Let Me Down • Drive My Car • Get Back • Good Day Sunshine • Hello, Goodbye • Hey Jude • In My Life • Lady Madonna.
00695650..$22.95

LENNON & MCCARTNEY FAVORITES
by Todd Lowry

16 more hits (L-Z) from The Beatles: Let It Be • The Long and Winding Road • Lucy in the Sky with Diamonds • Martha My Dear • Ob-La-Di, Ob-La-Da • Oh! Darling • Penny Lane • Revolution 9 • Rocky Raccoon • She's a Woman • Strawberry Fields Forever • We Can Work It Out • With a Little Help from My Friends • The Word • You're Going to Lose That Girl • Your Mother Should Know.
00695651..$22.95

BEST OF ROCK
by Todd Lowry

12 songs are analyzed: Bloody Well Right (Supertramp) • Cold as Ice (Foreigner) • Don't Do Me Like That (Tom Petty & The Heartbreakers) • Don't Let the Sun Go Down on Me (Elton John) • I'd Do Anything for Love (Meat Loaf) • Killer Queen (Queen) • Lady Madonna (The Beatles) • Light My Fire (The Doors) • Piano Man (Billy Joel) • Point of No Return (Kansas) • Separate Ways (Journey) • Werewolves of London (Warren Zevon).
00695751..$19.95

BEST OF ROCK 'N' ROLL PIANO
by David Bennett Cohen

12 of the best hits for piano are presented in this pack. Songs include: At the Hop • Blueberry Hill • Brown-Eyed Handsome Man • Charlie Brown • Great Balls of Fire • Jailhouse Rock • Lucille • Rock and Roll Is Here to Stay • Runaway • Tutti Frutti • Yakety Yak • You Never Can Tell.
00695627..$19.95

BEST OF STEVIE WONDER
by Todd Lowry

This book/CD pack includes musical examples, lessons, biographical notes, and more for 14 of Stevie Wonder's best songs. Features: I Just Called to Say I Love You • My Cherie Amour • Part Time Lover • Sir Duke • Superstition • You Are the Sunshine of My Life • and more.
00695605..$22.95

The Keyboard Play-Along series will help you quickly and easily play your favorite songs as played by your favorite artists. Just follow the music in the book, listen to the CD to hear how the keyboard should sound, and then play along using the separate backing tracks. The melody and lyrics are also included in the book in case you want to sing, or simply to help you follow along. The audio CD is playable on any CD player. For PC and Mac users, the CD is enhanced so you can adjust the recording to any tempo without changing pitch! Each book/CD pack in this series features eight great songs.

1. POP/ROCK HITS

Against All Odds (Take a Look at Me Now) (Phil Collins) • Deacon Blues (Steely Dan) • (Everything I Do) I Do It for You (Bryan Adams) • Hard to Say I'm Sorry (Chicago) • Kiss on My List (Hall & Oates) • My Life (Billy Joel) • Walking in Memphis (Marc Cohn) • What a Fool Believes (The Doobie Brothers).
00699875 Keyboard Transcriptions..$14.95

2. SOFT ROCK

Don't Know Much (Aaron Neville) • Glory of Love (Peter Cetera) • I Write the Songs (Barry Manilow) • It's Too Late (Carole King) • Just Once (James Ingram) • Making Love Out of Nothing at All (Air Supply) • We've Only Just Begun (Carpenters) • You Are the Sunshine of My Life (Stevie Wonder).
00699876 Keyboard Transcriptions..$12.95

3. CLASSIC ROCK

Against the Wind (Bob Seger) • Come Sail Away (Styx) • Don't Do Me like That (Tom Petty and the Heartbreakers) • Jessica (Allman Brothers) • Say You Love Me (Fleetwood Mac) • Takin' Care of Business (Bachman-Turner Overdrive) • Werewolves of London (Warren Zevon) • You're My Best Friend (Queen).
00699877 Keyboard Transcriptions..$14.95

4. CONTEMPORARY ROCK

Angel (Sarah McLachlan) • Beautiful (Christina Aguilera) • Because of You (Kelly Clarkson) • Don't Know Why (Norah Jones) • Fallin' (Alicia Keys) • Listen to Your Heart (D.H.T.) • A Thousand Miles (Vanessa Carlton) • Unfaithful (Rihanna).
00699878 Keyboard Transcriptions..$12.95

5. ROCK HITS

Back at One (Brian McKnight) • Brick (Ben Folds) • Clocks (Coldplay) • Drops of Jupiter (Tell Me) (Train) • Home (Michael Buble) • 100 Years (Five for Fighting) • This Love (Maroon 5) • You're Beautiful (James Blunt)
00699879 Keyboard Transcriptions..$14.95

6. ROCK BALLADS

Bridge over Troubled Water (Simon & Garfunkel) • Easy (Commodores) • Hey Jude (Beatles) • Imagine (John Lennon) • Maybe I'm Amazed (Paul McCartney) • A Whiter Shade of Pale (Procol Harum) • You Are So Beautiful (Joe Cocker) • Your Song (Elton John).
00699880 Keyboard Transcriptions..$14.95

More Volumes Coming Soon, Including:
Vol. 7 Rock Classics

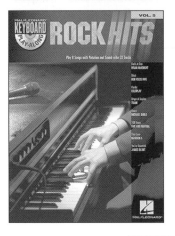

FOR MORE INFORMATION,
SEE YOUR LOCAL MUSIC DEALER,
OR WRITE TO:

HAL•LEONARD®
CORPORATION
7777 W. BLUEMOUND RD. P.O. BOX 13819
MILWAUKEE, WISCONSIN 53213

Visit Hal Leonard Online at **www.halleonard.com**

Prices, contents, and availability subject to change without notice.

0707